W9-DGX-585

◆ ◆

FOREWORD
by JOHN GRAY, Ph.D.,
author of *Men Are from Mars, Women Are from Venus*

I am delighted that my extraterrestrial stories about men and women have been expanded to explain nonhuman behaviors as well.

As we make peace with our human partners, it also makes sense to work toward a greater understanding of our cats and dogs. Who better to comfort us in tough times than our ever-patient, ever-loving fluffy or furry friends? They give us just the attention we need; the least we can do is try to understand where they are coming from.

How fortunate for us that Paul Reed has unlocked the secrets behind the seemingly strange behaviors of our favorite pets. Once we understand what life was like on Jupiter, cat behavior makes perfect sense. And when we see how differently the phrase "a dog's life" was interpreted on Pluto, we can much better understand the heretofore baffling behavior of the dogs in our lives. (You may want to read this book aloud to any feline or canine friends who share your home. Not only will you enjoy each new insight, your cat or dog will greatly appreciate the effort you're making to understand things from the four-footed perspective.)

Most important, whether dealing with cats, dogs, or humans, a sense of humor can make the difference between unbearable frustration and instant relief. Humor brings renewed patience that can help any relationship flourish. This book offers a unique perspective on cats and dogs that is sure to bring broad smiles, loud purrs, and strong tail wags to any species of Earthling that reads it.

A
COMMUNICATION
GUIDE
FOR
HUMANS

by
PAUL REED

Cartoons by MARK PARISI

FOREWORD BY
John Gray
author of *Men Are from Mars, Women Are from Venus*

Cats Are From Jupiter, Dogs Are From Pluto

POCKET BOOKS

New York   London   Toronto   Sydney   Tokyo   Singapore

An *Original* Publication of POCKET BOOKS

POCKET BOOKS, a division of Simon & Schuster Inc.
1230 Avenue of the Americas, New York, NY 10020

Copyright © 1994 by Patti Breitman and Paul Reed

ISBN: 0-671-52002-4

First Pocket Books trade paperback printing November 1994

10 9 8 7 6 5 4 3 2 1

POCKET and colophon are registered trademarks of
Simon & Schuster Inc.

Cover and interior illustrations by John Nickle
Text design by Stanley S. Drate/Folio Graphics Co., Inc.

Printed in the U.S.A.

CONTENTS

◆ v ◆

♦ ♦

ACKNOWLEDGMENTS

I thank my agent and packager, Patti Breitman, for having the nerve to ask me to develop this book with her, and for her expert guidance and keen editorial eye. I thank my friend Matt for boosting my enthusiasm. His support and confidence inspired me to write even when I didn't want to.

Writing this book gave me the opportunity to reflect on all the love that pets have provided throughout my lifetime. We don't remember our pets that have passed over to the other side as often as we remember the good times with Grandma or Grandpa, for example. And so I want to dedicate this book to the loving memory of my late cat Peggy (who provided so many examples of cat conduct discussed in this book), and to the memory of Fawn, Smoky, Duncan, Jaws, Calamity, and a number of miscellaneous goldfish. And I thank all the other wonderful pets around me for inspiration and guidance: Bill's dogs Ranger and Hunter; Berta's dog Shemp and cats Coco, Chanel, and Ixa; and Jim and Joe's dogs Christopher and Christina.

And I thank my mechanic, without whose bills I might never have had the motivation to press on with the project.

—Paul Reed

✦ ✦ ✦ ✦ ✦ ✦ ✦ ✦ ✦ ✦ ✦ ✦ ✦ ✦ ✦ ✦ ✦ ✦ ✦

INTRODUCTION

There's nothing that compares to that first time you bring home a sweet little kitten, full of love and friskiness, or when you bring home an adorable puppy, so innocent and playful. Instinctively you know that this is just the beginning of a long and loving relationship that will enrich your life—and the lives of your animal companions.

But like any relationship, having a pet has its high points and its low points, with a depth and complexity that can be both very rewarding and extremely annoying. The painful aspects of pet ownership are often rooted in misunderstanding. What cats and dogs actually think and feel is frequently very different from what we, as humans, perceive.

In time, this communication gap can become fixed and unyielding, like a hard-boiled egg. Over the years we develop viewpoints about our pets that actually become denial and codependence that can rob us of the full appreciation of our furry friends from the animal kingdom.

Such patterns need to be changed. The challenges of today's cold and uncaring society demand that we develop a clearer understanding of little Mittens and frisky Spot. When we learn how better to understand and communicate with our cats and dogs, we open ourselves to experience the profound richness of these interspecies relationships.

Cats Are from Jupiter, Dogs Are from Pluto is a manual for understanding and loving our animal companions. It shows how cats and dogs really think. Not only do cats and dogs communicate differently with humans than with each other, but they feel, react, perceive, need, and love differently. They almost seem to be from different planets!

CATS ARE
FROM
JUPITER,
DOGS ARE
FROM
PLUTO

1 | CATS ARE FROM JUPITER

Long before the time of recorded human history, cats began migrating to Earth from Jupiter. They were immediately loved by the primitive Earthlings and adopted as pets. There was no domestication involved; having humans take care of them was one of the reasons cats came to Earth, as we shall see.

To understand cats more fully, it's helpful to examine Jupiterian mythology, especially their myth of origin. (While humans generally use the word "Jovian" as an adjective to describe anything to do with Jupiter, cats actually prefer "Jupiterian," as that is their proper home planet terminology. "Jovian" was derived from human mythology much, much later.)

THE JUPITERIAN CREATION STORY

Vast and gaseous, the planet Jupiter has a diameter of more than 90,000 miles. The atmosphere of Jupiter is some 37,000 miles deep, surrounding a core of rock and iron.

A very large, very fat, and very furry female cat with nine huge tails rose from the chemical interaction between the planet's core and its mantle of gas.

Known as Queen Fluffy, this first cat-creature swam through Jupiter's atmosphere and began to meditate and purr very steadily. As a result of her purring, the many elements of the entire universe began to come together suddenly and form a sort of mechanistic rhythm and stabilizing vibration.

As Queen Fluffy practiced her meditative purring, one by one her tails fell off, until she had only one. But wherever each tail fell, another cat sprang to life.

And began to purr. Clearly there was some grand creative force at work here. Of course, Queen Fluffy understood it all—for she had been the first to be "created" by the grand creative force and charged with the task of keeping the harmonic vibrations going.

The Jupiterians were fruitful and multiplied, and it wasn't many millennia until it was discovered that overpopulation was threatening the planet.

For eons, Jupiterians were content to float around in this gassy atmosphere, performing their duties in the universal scheme of things—until this problem of overpopulation became critical.

It was then that Queen Fluffy—by now enormously ancient and wise—decreed that all the Jupiterian population should be split, in order to save them all. Half the cats would have to emigrate to another planet.

By this time, the powerful telescopes of Jupiter revealed that Earthlings were now advanced enough to be of some assistance in helping the immigrant Jupiterians adjust to a new planetary environment. So the first spaceships from Jupiter were dispatched to Earth.

It was a spectacular success, for the Earthlings immediately fell in love with the Jupiterians, hugging them close, feeding them, enjoying their warm and soft fluffiness, and being especially fascinated with the soothing vibrational sound the Jupiterians made.

Cats discovered that it was much easier to focus on their work when they didn't have to bother taking care of themselves. If they could have their meals and other needs provided by the Earthlings, they could devote nearly all their time to their work.

So in her infinite wisdom, Her Supreme Fluffiness, Queen Fluffy, decreed that the Earth-Jupiter alliance be formally, and eternally, formed.

Eventually, the Earthlings completely forgot that cats had actually come from outer space, though many modern mysteries are easily explained by the Jupiterian migration.

+ + + + + + + + + + + + + + + + + + + +
# Cats Come Running at the Sound of
# Electric Can Openers
+ + + + + + + + + + + + + + + + + + + +

For example, cats always come running when they hear the sound of an electric can opener. This often baffles humans, because it occurs even among cats who've never been fed canned food. But the whirring sound of the can opener reminds cats of the sound of the spaceships that shuttle cats back and forth between Jupiter and Earth.

+ + + + + + + + + + + + + + + + + + + +
# UFO Sightings Are Very Real
+ + + + + + + + + + + + + + + + + + + +

A little-known fact is that UFO sightings are very real—they are the vehicles of Jupiter Express, the interplanetary shuttle service running cats back and forth. The famous and mysterious lines on the Nazca Plain are, obviously, landing sights for the Jupiter Express, as are many other landmarks that have baffled modern scientists, such as the great pyramids of Egypt and Mexico, and the mysterious English crop circles.

This also explains why, sometimes, cats seem to disappear, stay-

ing out all night or even for a day or two. No matter how many times their names are called, they just don't come running. It's because they've caught a UFO shuttle home to Jupiter for a family visit or other business.

And the business of cats is very, very serious, as we shall see in the next chapter.

2 | WHAT CATS REALLY DO ALL DAY

It's neither love nor money that makes the world go around. It's cats. Their purring is in actuality the vibrational harmonic that binds together the matter and energy of the universe.

For centuries, humans have jested about the seemingly simple and luxurious lives of cats—that all they do is sleep most of the day, eat, mate, and sleep most of the night.

✦ ✦ ✦ ✦ ✦ ✦ ✦ ✦ ✦ ✦ ✦ ✦ ✦ ✦ ✦ ✦ ✦
Cats Do Not Actually Sleep All the Time
✦ ✦ ✦ ✦ ✦ ✦ ✦ ✦ ✦ ✦ ✦ ✦ ✦ ✦ ✦ ✦ ✦

But cats are not actually sleeping, even though they appear to be in deep slumber with their eyes closed. Cats are in fact the most intelligent beings in the known universe, and they spend the bulk of their time figuring out extraordinarily complex mathematical equations and calculating advanced physics and trigonometric equations that would boggle the mind of the most learned university professor.

As we discovered in the last chapter, cats were charged with the universal task of stabilizing the rotations of planets and the movements of the stars and other worlds by emitting vibrational humming at very precise pitches. Thus was born the practice of purring, a form of meditation that creates the harmony of the universe.

If cats are observed closely when in their various meditative states—bearing in mind their true work—it becomes quite obvious that they are practically in a trance as they contemplate serious scientific problems.

✦ ✦ ✦ ✦ ✦ ✦ ✦ ✦ ✦ ✦ ✦ ✦ ✦ ✦ ✦ ✦ ✦ ✦ ✦

It's Dangerous to Distract Cats

✦ ✦ ✦ ✦ ✦ ✦ ✦ ✦ ✦ ✦ ✦ ✦ ✦ ✦ ✦ ✦ ✦ ✦ ✦

This is why cats hate to be disturbed. In fact, it is even rather dangerous to distract cats at any time, because the universe could tilt dangerously off base if their Jupiterian equations are interrupted.

THE INFLUENCE OF CATS ON MODERN PHYSICS.

3 | UNDERSTANDING JUPITERIAN BEHAVIOR

Now that we understand what cats really do all day, we can see that cats are quite preoccupied all the time. This fact is central to cat psychology.

The way a cat behaves has roots in Jupiterian life. In ancient times, before cats journeyed from Jupiter to Earth, they built a vast academic culture and communicated with one another telepathically.

They brought their telepathic powers with them to Earth, but most humans are no longer sensitive enough—in this busy, distracting world—to pick up on the Jupiterian wavelength.

Humans knew more about this in ancient times. That's why cats were worshipped in Ancient Egypt, and why they have often been associated with witches down through the ages. Black cats, with their arched backs, hairs on end, and extended claws, play a special role in our perception of mystery and spiritual secrets.

THE ANCIENT EGYPTIANS, KNOWN TO ADORE CATS, WOULD OFTEN WORSHIP *THE FELINE DEITY* KNOWN AS "*EETANSLEEP AWLDAY.*"

But we humans have lost our own ability to receive telepathic, intuitive communication from our cats. Modern life, with its rushing around, its blaring televisions, and howling car alarms, has all but drowned out the subtle thought waves and messages that little Whiskers and Mittens are trying to send us.

Therefore, cats have had to develop a number of adaptive behaviors designed to communicate with humans in simple, unmistakable ways. Well, they were originally intended to be unmistakable, but over time these behaviors have, of course, become utterly misinterpreted. That's why we need to study Jupiterian behavior, so that we can get at the true meaning of cat conduct.

Leading such lofty intellectual lives—forever lost in thought, contemplation, and analysis—cats are easily startled. The sayings "nervous as a cat" or "jumpy as a kitten" reflect this trait.

✦ ✦ ✦ ✦ ✦ ✦ ✦ ✦ ✦ ✦ ✦ ✦ ✦ ✦ ✦ ✦ ✦ ✦

Forever Lost in Thought, Contemplation, and Analysis, Cats Are Easily Startled

✦ ✦ ✦ ✦ ✦ ✦ ✦ ✦ ✦ ✦ ✦ ✦ ✦ ✦ ✦ ✦ ✦ ✦

Cats require long hours of undisturbed silence in which to perform their analyses and mathematical equations. If paid too much atten-

tion—or too little—cats become ornery and cantankerous. When that happens, a precious fluffball can become a nasty, grumpy thorn in the flesh.

Therefore, the first key to understanding Jupiterian behavior is to realize that the cat is supreme—her needs must always come first. Or, at least, you must lead her to believe that her wish is your command.

Being so much farther from the sun, both days and nights on Jupiter are much, much longer than on Earth. Because of this, cats have evolved the ability to work with or without daylight. Whatever suits their mood.

✦ ✦ ✦ ✦ ✦ ✦ ✦ ✦ ✦ ✦ ✦ ✦ ✦ ✦ ✦ ✦ ✦ ✦ ✦ ✦

Cats Prefer Flextime

✦ ✦ ✦ ✦ ✦ ✦ ✦ ✦ ✦ ✦ ✦ ✦ ✦ ✦ ✦ ✦ ✦ ✦ ✦ ✦

For this reason, cats insist on flextime. This is unbendable. If Mittens wants to tear through the length of your house at three in the morning because she must test a theory regarding velocity and temporality, then you must simply heave a sigh of resignation. Do not attempt to interfere with her experiment, because she will only find another way to do it, at another time, perhaps even less convenient.

✦ ✦ ✦ ✦ ✦ ✦ ✦ ✦ ✦ ✦ ✦ ✦ ✦ ✦ ✦ ✦ ✦ ✦ ✦ ✦

Cats Are Quite Precise in Their Demands

✦ ✦ ✦ ✦ ✦ ✦ ✦ ✦ ✦ ✦ ✦ ✦ ✦ ✦ ✦ ✦ ✦ ✦ ✦ ✦

Food and sleep. Commit those two basics of life to memory and you will never be able to misinterpret Kitty's motives, desires, wants, or needs. Let's look at an example:

Whiskers is a large, long-haired mixed breed just entering young adulthood. She is quite devoted to her work, and spends long hours lost in contemplation. Her human "parents," Sue Ellen and John, often feel that Whiskers is distant, less frisky, and less attentive than when she was a kitten. They try to interest her in other things—cat toys, a scratching post, even a multitiered carpeted "castle."

Despite their efforts and expenditures, Whiskers remains aloof. Sue Ellen and John shrug their shoulders and attempt to accept that their precious kitten has changed.

What's going on here? Well, Whiskers isn't interested in cat toys or fancy castles. Whiskers just wants to be fed—very well fed, with the latest gourmet cat food—and then left alone to ponder the myster-

ies of the universe. The more that Sue Ellen and John place demands on Whiskers's time—rather than simply provide her with all the food she can eat and the solitude to enjoy it—Whiskers has no choice but to withdraw to create the space she needs.

The lesson, of course, that Whiskers is trying to communicate is that her cat bowl should be filled at all times. And that she requires twenty-one hours of sleep each day.

◆ ◆ ◆ ◆ ◆ ◆ ◆ ◆ ◆ ◆ ◆ ◆ ◆ ◆ ◆ ◆ ◆ ◆ ◆

𝕋he Goal of All Cat Behavior at All Times Is Comfort

◆ ◆ ◆ ◆ ◆ ◆ ◆ ◆ ◆ ◆ ◆ ◆ ◆ ◆ ◆ ◆ ◆ ◆ ◆

The basic rule, then, of Jupiterian psychology, is that the goal of all cat behavior at all times is comfort. All cat behavior is geared toward easy and direct gratification. Whether it's flextime or feeding time, Jupiterians are so devoted to the life of the intellect that they organize their lives—and their planet—around the principles of comfort.

As humans, the key to understanding what Kitty is up to is to assess what would make Kitty more comfortable at any given moment.

INTERPRETING JUPITERIAN BEHAVIOR

Cat Behavior	What Humans Think It Means	What the Cat Means
Rubbing ankles and purring loudly	"Kitty is glad to see me."	"Feed me, you bimbo."
♦ ♦ ♦		
Clawing at the new sofa	"Kitty needs to sharpen her claws."	"These people have lousy taste in furniture."
♦ ♦ ♦		
Spreading cat litter all over the floor around the cat box	"Kitty's trying to cover her business and doesn't understand she's not outdoors."	"What unholy conditions! How unsanitary! How embarassing!"
♦ ♦ ♦		
Refusing to budge from your lap	"Kitty is so comfortable and loves me so much."	"Leave me alone. You exist only to take care of me. You're a human heating pad."
♦ ♦ ♦		
Meowing loudly at the crack of dawn	"Kitty wants her breakfast."	"Feed me, you bimbo."

Cat Behavior	What Humans Think It Means	What the Cat Means
Staying out all night and not coming when you call	"Kitty has wandered too far. I hope she's okay."	"Worry yourself into a codependent frenzy! See if I care!"
✦ ✦ ✦		
Licking their paws and constantly grooming themselves	"Cats are so concerned with hygiene, such clean animals!"	"I'm making sure that there's plenty of fur spread all over the house!"
✦ ✦ ✦		
Kneading your stomach in preparation to have a nap	"Kitty is nesting and thinks she's preparing a soft bed."	"Aren't you hungry yet? Don't forget to feed me!"
✦ ✦ ✦		
Batting at the newspaper when you're trying to read it	"Kitty's feeling frisky."	"Turn to the page with the coupons for cat food!"

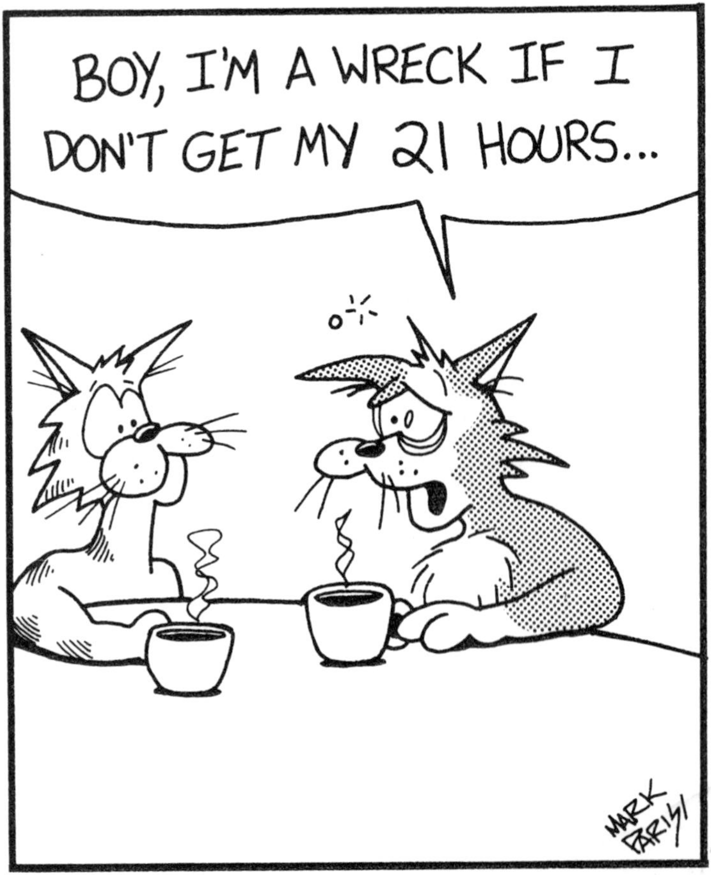
BOY, I'M A WRECK IF I DON'T GET MY 21 HOURS...
MARK PARISI

4 | COMMUNICATING WITH KITTY

It is nearly impossible for humans to master the Jupiterian language, called "Meowese." The human vocal apparatus is not properly equipped to deal with kitty-cat sounds. But cats have absolutely no trouble interpreting human language. They are, however, ultrasensitive to the level of respect and dignity with which they are treated.

And they have certain sensitive areas—they do not like to be commanded to do, or not do, anything. Since they consider themselves to be the ultimately evolved living form, it is best to play on their sensitivities in order to get them to behave in certain ways.

The following chart offers a few examples:

♦ ♦

COMMON MISTAKES IN COMMUNICATING WITH CATS

Don't say:	*Do Say:*
"Don't claw the furniture"	"Clawing furniture makes me so mad that I completely forget about feeding you."
♦ ♦ ♦	
"Here, kitty, kitty, kitty!"	"Get in here if you want any dinner."
♦ ♦ ♦	
"Could you get off my lap, because my leg's going to sleep."	"I think there are some tuna treats in the other room."
♦ ♦ ♦	
"Stop wailing, it's only six o'clock in the morning."	"If I don't get enough sleep, I'll be too drowsy to remember your breakfast."
♦ ♦ ♦	
"Get down from there!"	"Didn't I just fill your cat bowl with shrimps and crabmeat?"
♦ ♦ ♦	
"I love you."	"Would you like some catnip?"

5 | A MEOWESE TRANSLATOR

Meowese is more than just a language. It is a complex communication system that includes verbal, nonverbal, and telepathic elements. Here is a brief overview of some of the basic vocabulary of Meowese:

Meowese	Human Translation
Standard meow	"Hello. How are you?"
♦ ♦ ♦	
Forceful meow	"Hey, pay attention! Scratch behind my ears. Feed me!"
♦ ♦ ♦	
Purr	This is the work cats do to hold the fabric of the universe together.

Meowese	*Human Translation*
Whimper	"Please feel sorry for me and give me anything I want."
✦ ✦ ✦	
Hiss	"Feed me right now, you bimbo!"
✦ ✦ ✦	
Yowl	"I need a date!"
✦ ✦ ✦	
Squeak	"Chess, anyone?"
✦ ✦ ✦	
Tail whip	"I'm not happy with this situation, not in the least. Watch your figurines."
✦ ✦ ✦	
Arched back	"Get back! You look like my gnarly great-aunt Bootsy!"
✦ ✦ ✦	
Arched back with hiss	"Watch it! You're about to mess with a direct descendant of Queen Fluffy!"

⑥ TROUBLE SIGNS

Cats require a tremendous amount of attention. This may seem odd, given the fact that their work gives the appearance of slumber most of the time. Also, their seeming love of solitude is often misinterpreted to mean that Kitty wants to be left alone, if not ignored altogether.

But cats can become deeply troubled if they don't receive constant evidence that humans are devoted to the well-being of their cats. Listed below are the seven warning signs that indicate a cat's faltering sense of security.

THE SEVEN WARNING SIGNS THAT KITTY IS BECOMING UPSET

1. Kitty yowls ceaselessly at half past four in the morning.
2. Kitty whips her tail around so hard that it knocks over your precious porcelain, ceramics, and crystal.

3. Kitty sheds enough fur on your lap to stuff a pillow.
4. Kitty occupies most of the available bed space at night and will not budge.
5. Kitty digs her claws into your thighs when settling in for a nap.
6. Kitty makes a habit of barfing up fur balls on the couch.
7. Kitty "sprays" on your new shoes when they're sitting in the closet.

In the next chapter we'll take a look at the things that can be done to boost Kitty's self-esteem and maintain her sense of satisfaction, and reassure cats that they are of the utmost importance in humans' lives.

7 | SCORING POINTS WITH CATS

1. Feed them regularly.
2. Leave them alone to get their twenty-one hours of "sleep" (work) a day.
3. Keep plenty of catnip on hand.
4. Grow long fingernails to scratch behind their ears.
5. Train your houseguests not to shoo them off the dinner table.
6. Hang drapes low enough that little Whiskers, Kitty, or Mittens can claw them easily.
7. Never name them Whiskers, Kitty, or Mittens.
8. Reupholster all the furniture on a regular basis to provide fresh scratching opportunities.
9. Feed them frequently.
10. Let them in and out immediately whenever they meow, even if only a few seconds have passed.

11. Never dress them in little sweaters.
12. Never hang little bells from their collars.
13. Change the litter box frequently.
14. Never serve dry food, only the fancy canned varieties.
15. Forbid usage of the word "catty" in their presence. Cats consider this term to be highly derogatory.
16. Never, ever brush out their coats.
17. Keep houseplants readily accessible for digging up.
18. Get new goldfish on a regular basis.
19. Be sure they receive plenty of presents—little balls or squeeze toys, for example. These aid them in their scientific experiments.
20. Feed them constantly.

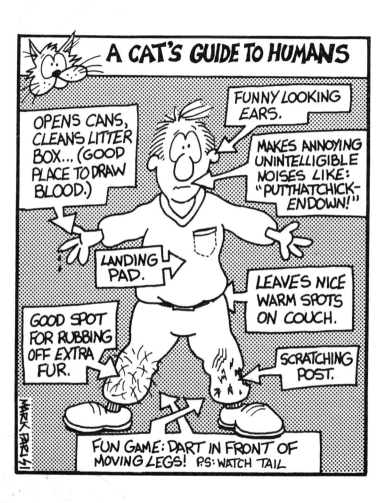

8 | DOGS ARE FROM PLUTO

Pluto is more than three and a half billion miles from the sun. Being so far out on the edge of the solar system, it is very cold and dark on Pluto. Plutonians, then, have always tended toward loneliness, grown great coats of soft, thick fur, and placed a high value on daylight.

◆ ◆ ◆ ◆ ◆ ◆ ◆ ◆ ◆ ◆ ◆ ◆ ◆ ◆ ◆ ◆ ◆ ◆ ◆ ◆

They Came from the Very Edge of the Solar System

◆ ◆ ◆ ◆ ◆ ◆ ◆ ◆ ◆ ◆ ◆ ◆ ◆ ◆ ◆ ◆ ◆ ◆ ◆ ◆

When, eons ago, they discovered how much closer to the sun Earth is, and how many living things thrived on Earth, there was no question that vast numbers of Pluto's citizens would emigrate to Earth.

ANCESTRY OF EARTH-DWELLING DOGS

Long ago, as the citizens of Pluto developed higher and higher forms of technology, the great scientist Doctor Fido invented a powerful telescope that could see clear across the solar system and into the Milky Way (which Plutonians called the "Milkbone Way").

There was a great flurry of discovery, the most exciting of which was a planet quite close to home, one covered with green forests, blue seas, and puffy white clouds. On closer examination, they saw that this planet was home to many species of wild animals, from the tiniest creatures to tall, gangly creatures who stumbled about on two spindly limbs.

They also observed that the spindly limbed creatures lavished great attention and devoted great care to small four-legged creatures covered in soft fur, who seemed to be revered as the highest form of living being.

The Plutonians—in their cold, dark world—resolved to journey to this distant planet. It was much closer to the sun, and hence brighter and warmer. And they were sure they could befriend the fur-ball creatures and charm the spindly limbed beings into taking care of them as well.

So off they went, emigrating to Earth. But it didn't go quite as planned. Even though the spindly limbs were immediately charmed by the Plutonian dogs, the Jupiterian cats were naturally resentful of these outlandish creatures—usually bigger than them-

OOOO, TREES EVERYWHERE! NOW IF WE CAN JUST TRAIN THE NATIVES TO SCRATCH OUR BELLIES WE'RE IN BUSINESS!
MARK PARISI

selves—who were trying to horn in on their turf. Rude and vulgar and common—this is how the Jupiterian cats perceived the Plutonian dogs. Dogs were noisy and overly energetic, interfering with the solitude and silence necessary for cats to perform their important work.

So was born a natural enmity between the emigrants from Jupiter and Pluto, a tension that exists to this day.

9 | THE MEANING OF A DOG'S LIFE

A dog's sense of success is defined by providing good company and faithful service. If they can gain the attention of their companions—be it other dogs, humans, or cats—dogs feel fulfilled.

Now, when the universe was being created, dogs got a pretty good deal. Unlike cats, whose purring and scientific skills landed them the job of maintaining the universal balance, dogs were pretty much left to their own devices. Which means, of course, that they developed an interest in feeling good, playing, just meeting their simple needs for food, rest, and mating.

This is another reason that cats don't like dogs very much—cats feel that dogs are lazy and somewhat useless. But of course, everything in life needs balance, and the happy-go-lucky, laid-back nature of dogs is the natural complement to the intensity of cat-work.

◆ ◆

Cats Feel That Dogs Are Lazy and Somewhat Useless

◆ ◆

So, in fact, dogs fulfill a vital role in the scheme of things, helping to achieve a universal balance between work and play. A dog's life consists, therefore, of activities primarily related to lightheartedness, playfulness, and simple pleasure.

This is the meaning of a dog's life—to spread joy and simplicity. Of course, human history has taken a turn toward workaholism and denial, and so we have defined "a dog's life" as meaning a life of drabness and misery. But nothing could be further from the truth. On Pluto, when the phrase "a dog's life" is used, it is a high form of flattery.

In the next chapter we'll examine how dog psychology is rooted in this commitment to joviality, and some of the reasons these characteristics emerged on the planet Pluto.

10 | PLUTONIC PSYCHOLOGY

$\mathbb{B}$ecause Pluto is so far away, so cold, and so very dark, Plutonians actually have a natural tendency toward loneliness, and suffer a slightly melancholy mood under the surface. Therefore, as we've seen, they've developed certain skills necessary to compensate for this natural mopiness—socializing, friendship, a love of light and warmth, and companionship. Dogs are always endeavoring to brighten the world around them.

* * * * * * * * * * * * * * * * * * * *

$\mathbb{P}$lutonians Tend Toward Loneliness

* * * * * * * * * * * * * * * * * * * *

Also because of this, dogs tend to be somewhat overbearing. We'll take a closer look at these dynamics in the case of Rover:

Rover, an easygoing collie in his late youth, suddenly developed a certain penchant for barking at all hours of the day or night. It was nothing fierce, just continuous. His human family members became alarmed—what was wrong? What was Rover trying to communicate? Was he ill? Was it cancer? Weight gain? Perhaps unresolved childhood issues or even the onset of a depression? Might Rover become suicidal? Or turn vicious?

Visits to the vet, blood tests, and exams yielded no evidence of anything wrong. They tried therapy, taking Rover to one of the most respected dog psychiatrists in town. But the dog shrink had very little success. Rover just kept on barking.

What was happening here? How does this tell us something about the inner workings of the Plutonic mind? Well, it's really rather simple. Because their need to be noticed, loved, and involved in the social life around them is so very great (owing to the difficulties of life on Pluto), certain behaviors that can seem at times too rambunctious come rushing out. It's a genetically programmed mechanism to compensate for loneliness. Even the mere thought of loneliness is enough to set a dog off on a behavioral direction that is less than pleasing to humans.

In this case, Rover's human family took the usual route of searching for physical or mental clues as to Rover's state of health, suspecting that something was wrong. Something *was* wrong, but it was more a spiritual problem than anything else.

Because of our fast-paced, busy lives, we humans tend to be away from our homes for quite lengthy periods of time. Leaving Rover alone for hours and hours, for days on end, he was denied the fulfillment of a dog's life function: to entertain, to be of service, to be a friend. His misbehavior was a signal of the onset of a deep existential crisis.

It was the last dog therapist they tried who understood Rover's problem and prescribed a change of lifestyle for the entire family — so that Rover could receive the attention and perform the services he so needed in order to feel he was a useful and contributing member of society.

✦ ✦

The Pleasure Principle

✦ ✦

When viewed in the context of the differences between cats and dogs, we see that the main contrast between Jupiterians and Plutonians is that cats are so serious about their work that they've lost sight of what dogs strive for, namely, the "Pleasure Principle." Once we understand that dogs exist primarily to fulfill a destiny of fun and service to others, we begin to see how better to live with our dogs—and our cats, for that matter.

When dogs migrated from Pluto in ancient times, they created a phrase to describe themselves: "Man's best friend." (Unfortunately, this phrase reflects the days before male and female equality began to work its way into everyday language, but the idea remains the same—"People's best friend.")

The reason they did this was to instill a sense of their role in life, whether it be on Pluto or on Earth. Dogs are intended to be friends, companions, helpmates, and entertainers.

To this end, dogs are devoted to certain values: fun, chaos, simplicity, service, and obedience (such as fetching, guarding, entertaining with "dog tricks").

❖ ❖ ❖ ❖ ❖ ❖ ❖ ❖ ❖ ❖ ❖ ❖ ❖ ❖ ❖ ❖ ❖ ❖ ❖ ❖

The Goal of All Dog Behavior at All
Times Is the Promotion of Frivolity and
the Provision of Service

❖ ❖ ❖ ❖ ❖ ❖ ❖ ❖ ❖ ❖ ❖ ❖ ❖ ❖ ❖ ❖ ❖ ❖ ❖ ❖

Thus we see quite clearly that the basic rule of Plutonic psychology is to understand that dogs gear themselves toward service and fun. Whether it's time to fetch or time to guard or time to play ball, Pluto-

nians are so devoted to the pleasure principle that everything they do is organized around it.

As humans, the key to understanding what Doggy is up to is to assess what, in any given moment, would give Doggy the opportunity to create pleasure.

✦ ✦

INTERPRETING PLUTONIC BEHAVIOR

Dog Behavior	*What Humans Think It Means*	*What the Dog Means*
Shaking their heads and bodies when wet	"Doggy is trying to dry off."	"Yahoo, let's spread the fun around! And I might get a good towel rubdown out of this."
✦ ✦ ✦		
Hanging their heads out of cars while in motion	"Doggy sure does love excitement, and the feel of wind in his face!"	"Gee, this reminds me of the trip from Pluto. That sure was fun."
✦ ✦ ✦		
Sniffing other dogs' (or cats') hindquarters	"Dogs need to get the scent of an animal to understand it. It's like the human handshake. It's perfectly natural."	"This is the kinkiest thing I can get away with. It's amazing no one's ever caught on."

Dog Behavior	What Humans Think It Means	What the Dog Means
Circling round and round before finally settling in	"It's a nesting instinct, like burrowing in the snow or grass for warmth or protection."	"I have absolutely no idea why I'm doing this."
✦ ✦ ✦		
Humping legs	"Doggy's feeling awfully frisky!"	"I need a date, now!"
✦ ✦ ✦		
Getting in the trash and spreading it all over	"Dog's got the devil in 'em and got to act up. Probably looking for some bones and snacks."	"Wow, this is fun! Humans don't have near enough fun making messes."
✦ ✦ ✦		
Attraction to signposts, trees, and fire hydrants for "relief"	"Male dogs must mark their territory."	"Earthlings are so uncivilized, failing to provide us with a place to 'go.' Even those damn cats get litter boxes. Well, I'll show them!"
✦ ✦ ✦		
Burying bones	"Doggy's hiding his bone for future safekeeping."	"Jeez, don't people know enough to bury dead things?"

YOU NEVER FORGET YOUR FIRST LOVE.

11 | UNDERSTANDING "BOW-WOW"

As with Meowese, the Plutonic dog language, Bow-Wow, is comprised of verbal and nonverbal elements. Some of these are well understood by humans, but others—as shown below—are commonly misinterpreted.

Bow-Wow	Human Translation
Woof-woof (standard bark)	"How's it going? I'm feeling good."
◆ ◆ ◆	
Fierce bark	"Hey, if you're within the sound of this bark, pay attention to me. Immediately!"

Bow-Wow	Human Translation
Growl	"Who's disturbing my nap? I was in a good mood just a minute ago."
✦ ✦ ✦	
Yelp/whimper	"Anyone want to play fetch?"
✦ ✦ ✦	
Howl/"baying at the moon"	"I'm homesick. I want to go back to Pluto."
✦ ✦ ✦	
Panting	"These are my deep-breathing exercises. Goes with tail wagging."
✦ ✦ ✦	
Tail wagging	"And this is my low-impact aerobics."
✦ ✦ ✦	
Face licking	"Let's see if you're wearing makeup!"
✦ ✦ ✦	
Snarl	"The fun index is getting awfully low here, and you're definitely working my nerves. Better watch that there's not too much lapse in fun time."
✦ ✦ ✦	
Snarl with ears laid back	"Get away! You smell like a cat!"

LISTEN, BERTHA... I'M CHASING CATS TILL FOUR, CHEWING UP THE CARPETS TILL SIX, TIPPING GARBAGE CANS TILL NINE, LICKING MYSELF TILL ABOUT NINE-THIRTY AND BARKING CONSTANTLY STRAIGHT THROUGH THE NIGHT, SO TELL MR. "MASTER" MY BATH WILL HAVE TO BE RESCHEDULED...
MARK PARISI

12 TRAINING SPOT TO BEHAVE

There are many different approaches to training dogs, but none of them is completely effective, because they fail to take into account the "alien" nature of canine origins on Pluto.

Being so happy-go-lucky, dogs are not naturally inclined toward discipline, or even obedience, if it is enforced through the use of painful methods like swatting with rolled-up newspapers or yanking on leashes. Instilling discipline through punishment—punishment that relies on the infliction of physical pain, emotional pain, or deprivation of some sort—can be effective to a limited degree. But it is not something that dogs like. In fact, in the end, they'll probably rebel against human meanness and just run completely amok.

But as we've seen, dogs love to provide service, entertainment, and friendship to their human companions. The best way to train Spot to behave is to encourage him to do the things he loves best, to lure him into proper conduct rather than try to force him to behave in order to avoid some sort of unpleasantness.

❖ ❖

COMMON MISTAKES IN COMMUNICATING WITH DOGS

Don't Say:	*Do Say:*
"Stop barking, you'll wake the neighbors."	"You know, Mrs. Smith next door just loathes and despises cats."
❖ ❖ ❖	
"Stop digging up the garden! Those flowers cost money!"	"You're behaving just like a cat. Did you come from Jupiter by any chance?"
❖ ❖ ❖	
"Don't bite."	"Hands, arms, feet, and small children do not make good fetch toys."
❖ ❖ ❖	
"Don't hump the preacher's wife's leg!"	"The preacher's wife has fleas."
❖ ❖ ❖	
"Don't lick yourself there!"	"What's the matter? Couldn't find a real date?"

13 | SCORING POINTS WITH DOGS

Humans tend to think that they are scoring points and winning the loyal devotion of their dogs when they brush out their dog's fur or give them big hugs or play silly little toss and fetch games with them in the park.

But dogs look at it a little differently. Dogs grant the highest scores not for warm demonstrations of their owner's affection for them, but for greater and greater freedom to do as they please without all manner of reprimands and discipline. Hugs and hygiene are fine and dandy—but they don't win a dog's heart.

Here is a list of just a few things you can do to score high with your dog:

1. Let him scratch and chew the Oriental carpets.
2. Keep plenty "dog bone" treats on hand and don't be stingy with them.

3. Allow barking at three in the morning.
4. Don't discipline him for digging up the garden. Instead, laugh and giggle when you come home to find the flowers strewn across the lawn.
5. Never, ever bathe him.
6. Allow endless face licking, and tell them "Oh, your dog breath is so sweet."
7. Don't trim his fur like a French poodle's, with tufts around the ankles or neck, and a mohawk atop his head, especially if he is a French poodle.
8. Never put ribbons or bows on him. The same goes for sweaters, rhinestone collars, and fancy little lacey sweat-sock things.
9. Let him knock down garbage cans and small children.
10. Take him to the beach and let him run wild in the surf, and *then* let him get back in the car all wet and muddy and shake sand all over the clean upholstery. (He'll really love this!)
11. Let him lick himself to his heart's content, especially if he wants to do it in front of company, vigorously digging and sniffing as well.
12. Don't name him Fido, Rover, or Spot.
13. Get a cat and let him terrorize it endlessly.
14. Never use a leash.
15. Let him relieve himself on your neighbor's lawn.

FLUFFY GETS EVEN

14 | KEEPING THE MAGIC ALIVE

A mysterious component of all loving relationships is their fickle nature. Devoted companions suddenly seem distant. Or we find ourselves relishing a mean-spirited withholding of a beloved pet's supper, holding the bowl in midair just out of reach until Mittens or Fido raises enough of a fuss that we give in—but then find we're shocked by our seemingly inexplicable, unloving behavior. Perhaps you can relate to one or more of these examples:

1. One day, you suddenly find that Kitty's early-morning meowing is extraordinarily annoying to you, even though just yesterday you thought it was the sweetest, warmest, most loving sound in the world.
2. Just when you're so proud of Fido for finally learning to fetch the

newspaper, he chews the paper to shreds and drops it, spit-soaked, on your new shoes.

3. One evening, Mittens is so affectionate that you can't get her off your lap. In the morning, however, she turns her nose up at breakfast and promptly relieves herself on the beige carpet in the dining room.

4. Spot suddenly loses interest in leg humping. One day he won't leave anyone alone, yet the next day he's cold as ice.

The first thing to do about these situations and sudden shifts in mood is to understand that they are perfectly normal. Our emotions are quite volatile, and the same is true of these aliens among us. Life on Earth isn't easy, just as life on Jupiter or Pluto isn't easy.

By learning something of the background of cats and dogs, we grow more fully able to appreciate them in all their richness and fullness—including the bad times, when tensions mount. But by studying their myths and social customs, as this book has helped us do, by understanding their languages and nonverbal expressions, and by opening our minds to accept the realities of other worlds, we open our own human hearts and help create a more peaceful, loving, spiritual, and conscious world—and universe too. And in so doing, we soften any tensions between us, and soon enough we find that playful, loving feelings return.

We're all just plugging along, doing the best we can to fulfill our various life destinies. There is much to hope for, and to look forward to. We've barely begun to understand the mysteries of existence. Our pets can help us to learn and grow in awareness, understanding, and love.

Blessings!

For orders other than by individual consumers, Pocket Books grants a discount on the purchase of **10 or more** copies of single titles for special markets or premium use. For further details, please write to the Vice-President of Special Markets, Pocket Books, 1230 Avenue of the Americas, New York, NY 10020.

For information on how individual consumers can place orders, please write to Mail Order Department, Paramount Publishing, 200 Old Tappan Road, Old Tappan, NJ 07675.